The Rosary

Worry Beads for Anxious Parents

Patricia M. Robertson

ST. ANTHONY MESSENGER PRESS

Cincinnati, Ohio

Nihil Obstat: Hilarion Kistner, O.F.M.
Rev. Robert A. Stricker
Imprimi Potest: Fred Link, O.F.M.
Provincial
Imprimatur: +Most Reverend Carl K. Moeddel, V.G.
Archdiocese of Cincinnati
April 11, 2003

Scripture citations are taken from the *New Revised Standard
Version Bible*, copyright ©1989 by the Division of Christian
Education of the National Council of Churches of Christ in the
U.S.A. and used by permission.

Cover and book design by Mark Sullivan
Cover photo ©Patrick Sheandell O Carroll/PhotoAlto/PictureQuest

Library of Congress Cataloging-in-Publication Data

Robertson, Patricia M.
 The rosary : worry beads for anxious parents / Patricia M.
Robertson.
    p. cm.
 ISBN 0-86716-518-9
 1. Mysteries of the Rosary. 2. Parents—Prayer-books and
devotions—English. I. Title.
 BT303.R585 2003
 242'.74—dc21

                          2003007203

ISBN 0-86716-518-9
Published by St. Anthony Messenger Press
www.AmericanCatholic.org
Printed in the U.S.A.

Contents

INTRODUCTION

Webster defines *mystery* as something not understood, a problem or puzzle, an enigma, a Christian sacrament. Good mysteries are wonderful. They keep our attention, keep us wondering, keep us coming back for more until the denouement when all is explained, everything comes together and makes sense. When reading a mystery story I have to resist the urge to stay up all night reading in order to find out "whodunit." I have to discipline myself to take them in moderate amounts lest I neglect all of the daily responsibilities of life. And then when I've come to the last page of the story, I hate to have it end. I want the story to go on and on.

The wonderful thing about the mysteries of our faith is that they never end. You never close the book and say it's over, at least not while you live. You may reach ends of chapters but never the end of the story. The mystery goes on and on. For those who like closure and to have things explained, this can be extremely aggravating. For those who love mysteries, this open-endedness can add delight, wonder and not a little dramatic tension to our lives, as we watch to see how the mysteries play out. Mysteries can be problems to solve or dramas to unfold.

We have our role to fulfill in these mysteries. We are not simply readers of a book or part of the audience at a play. We are the actors and writers, taking part in a drama that began before any of us were born and that will continue after we are gone. For some, life may appear to be like a comedy, for others a romance and for others a tragedy. But all participate in the great mysteries of life.

The mysteries of faith that are part of the rosary give us ample room for reflection and wonder. My own understanding has changed tremendously over the years from when I first learned this prayer as a child. I remember lying awake then, waiting to fall asleep. As darkness enveloped the room, I felt my young mind threatened also to be enveloped by darkness, large and empty and scary. Thoughts of death, thoughts of destruction from news overheard on the TV, thoughts beyond my mind's capacity to comprehend threatened to keep me from sleep.

By grace I was led to pray. I was led to a prayer taught to me by my mother and the sisters at school. I found that when the dark thoughts threatened, if I said the rosary those thoughts receded back into the void from whence they had come. I found peace and sleep. Very rarely in those youthful days did I get past one or two decades before falling into a deep sleep. This didn't concern me. The sisters had said that if you fell asleep while praying the angels completed the prayer for you. So when I composed "spiritual bouquets" as gifts I confidently gave myself credit for a full rosary each night. I handcrafted cards listing all the prayers I had said for the important people in my life—my parents, my grandmother and a Methodist aunt, who probably had no idea what this crazy Catholic was doing, but who, I figured, would appreciate prayers regardless of the form they took.

Somewhere between childhood and adolescence I stopped saying this evening rosary. Perhaps it was because I fell asleep quickly and soundly after each busy day, or perhaps because my thoughts had taken on a different, more pleasant tone. Regardless of why, this nightly habit had been relegated to the past, to my childhood, like a security blanket or teddy bear I had out-grown. I no longer thought about this prayer until many years later when I was in my twenties and found myself awakened by nightmares I didn't remember but whose aftereffect lingered on through the small hours of the night. I found myself plagued by thoughts and fears that I was more capable of dealing with now as an adult, but which were still difficult thoughts that robbed me of sleep and peace of mind.

The previous summer I had spent in the Dominican Republic with some Dominican sisters who ministered among the campesinos in a mountain region. I love traveling and had traveled in Europe several times before but had never traveled to a developing country. The huge discrepancies between what we had as Americans and what the campesinos had, their tremendous poverty, had awakened a sense of outrage that I had not known existed inside me. It had been especially hard to see malnourished children and children with terrible burn scars from falling into campfires. This had awakened something in me that had led to the nightmares and the trouble sleeping.

I lay awake trying to sort things out and make sense of all this that made no sense at all. After a while I would figure I had done all I could at this time and would tell myself to let it be and go back to sleep. But, of course, the thoughts didn't turn themselves off so easily, and I continued to toss and turn. It was then that I remembered my youthful prayers and how praying the rosary had helped me get to sleep. I decided to give it a try. It didn't matter that I had no idea where my old rosary was. Conveniently I had ten fingers, which were all I needed to keep track of each decade.

The prayers didn't work as quickly as when I was younger. Sometimes I would work my way through all fifteen decades before sleep came. Still, the prayers helped me to get my mind off what was bothering me. As prayer, I figured it was good use of my time even if I didn't fall asleep right away. And although sleep did not always come immediately, I still felt a sense of peace afterward.

And so I renewed my acquaintance with the rosary, relegating it only to those nights that I was awakened by troublesome dreams, which fortunately did not happen too often.

In my late twenties and early thirties my children were born. Then my sleep was constantly disrupted by their night awakenings. At the least whimper I would jump out of bed to make sure all was well with them. With three children, there were nights when I would be up as many as eight to ten times. I longed for the days when they would sleep soundly through the night. Now that my children are long past the stage of waking me up each night, I'm still waking up. Old habits are hard to break.

I wake up and worry about all the things there are for a parent and church minister to worry about. I think about my children, what's going on in their lives. I think about my ministry, problems I encounter, people I'm concerned about. I think about myself and this crazy world we live in and I wonder what it is I am called to do. I try to understand.

Now the rosary has become a more regular prayer companion as once again I wake up in the middle of the night and can't get back to sleep. I often get through all twenty decades and still lie awake. But even if I don't get the sleep I'm hoping for, I'm much more peaceful after praying the rosary. The beads have become my worry beads as well as prayer beads. I pour my worries out into them.

The mysteries connected to the rosary have also become a great source for reflection for me on Mary's life, Jesus' life, the life of the early Christian community and my own life. I continue to see new connections and gain new insights that help me in my waking life. I anticipate with joy the mysteries of Jesus' birth and early years, as they bring back to me the joys of my own children's births. I don't necessarily look forward to the sorrowful mysteries, and yet I have found in them a source of great comfort when dealing with my own crosses in life. I've yet to grasp the glorious mysteries (not that I necessarily grasp the totality of the other mysteries). They seem to me to be for a future time I've yet to encounter. I have glimpses of that glory which is God's, but only glimpses. They are all the more glorious because of the preceding mysteries. Glory is beyond joy and light and beyond sorrow, and beyond me!

With the recent addition of the Mysteries of Light, I have more mysteries to reflect upon that enlighten my path through this journey of life. They give me greater insight into Jesus—who he was and continues to be.

The mysteries go on as I continue to find new meaning, new richness in each of them. They are enhanced by the many relationships God brings into my life—each with its own mystery. I look forward to their continued unfolding as I live out this mystery of my life.

The following meditations are the outgrowth of my nightly musings. My appreciation for this prayer of the church continues to grow and deepen as I grow in my own faith life. May they be a help for you in your own faith journey.

THE JOYFUL
MYSTERIES

FIRST JOYFUL MYSTERY
The Annunciation

*In the sixth month the angel Gabriel was sent
by God to a town in Galilee called Nazareth,
to a virgin engaged to a man whose name was
Joseph, of the house of David. The virgin's
name was Mary.—Luke 1:26–27*

A mere slip of a girl, a teenager, listens to an angelic messenger. Obviously, it takes a teenager to say such an unqualified "yes" to this strange messenger. Teenagers see only possibilities. The whole world lies before them with so little to compare anything to. Anything could happen in their eyes. Becoming a movie star or a rock star or a computer genius, a multi-millionaire before the age of twenty-five—all are possible. There is no limit to the imagination of teenagers. Teens would relish the idea of being specially chosen or having an angelic visitor. After all, they are the center of their own universe. Why shouldn't an angel of God come to them? But then again, why should an angel of God come to them? They are also full of youthful insecurities and uncertainties, often masked by a false sense of bravado.

Still, only a teenager, which Mary was, could say "yes" with such youthful abandon. What does she know? Does she have any idea what she is getting herself into? Did she stop to count the cost? Of course not. She was just a child. Little did she know what sacrifices being the mother of a savior would entail. I would have asked Gabriel to give me at least a week to think about it, pray about it, before giving an answer. I would have wanted a chance to talk this over with my fiancé. I would have wanted time to count the costs: What would Joseph say? What would the neighbors say? What would my parents say? Would I be left to deal with this pregnancy on my own or would they support me?

"Joseph, by the way, what would you think if I were suddenly to become pregnant and it was not your child? You see, I've got an offer I can't refuse . . ."

Certainly this was not a good way to begin a marriage. Mary just goes off on her own and makes this decision without consulting her soon-to-be husband. This type of decision-making has gotten more than one marriage into hot water. We talk about the family of Mary and Joseph and Jesus as a role model for families, but I have to wonder about this.

But then, of course, Joseph had his angelic visitor, as well. I wonder about this also. As hard as it was for Mary, wasn't it even harder for Joseph? Mary had the assurance that, if this were God's child she was bearing, certainly somehow it would have to work out. Mary knew whose the child was. Joseph had only Mary's word and the angel's word. Even with an angelic visitor I think I would have been tempted to doubt, to doubt this woman's word and my own perception. How much harder was it for Joseph? Did he wonder at times whose child Mary was carrying? It would seem only natural. As hard as it would be to marry someone who was carrying another man's child, it seems to me it would be harder to marry someone who claimed to be carrying God's child, because then you couldn't help but question whether she was telling you the truth. If this were so, where was the basis for any trust? Again, what a way to begin a marriage. Still, the gift of the angel to Joseph was to dispel the doubt and restore trust. Did Mary or Joseph really have any idea what they were getting themselves into? Do any of us truly know what we are getting ourselves into with our children? Even if we already have several children, each is unique and different from the others, challenging us to grow in different ways, requiring us to find new ways of loving each child. And so it is with each child that we are required to trust yet again, to trust that our God will help us through whatever challenges we may face, just as Mary and Joseph had to trust.

Part of the beauty of the Annunciation is that it is also the conception. In focusing on the angel and his message we often miss that. As hard as it is to imagine such a miraculous visitor and conception, as a mother I know what it is to conceive a child, to feel a sense of co-creation with our creator. I know what it is to feel a child stir within me and know that God is doing something great inside me. It is a wonder and a mystery.

I have used this passage in Scripture as a guided meditation for myself and for others. I encourage them to imagine themselves in that room with Mary as the angel Gabriel appears. I encourage them to imagine the angel turning to them—what might the angel say? Gabriel's message, "Fear not," is a tremendous source of strength and peace. Certainly, I am no Mary, and yet God does speak to me through angels he has sent into my life and through prayer.

When I reflect on this mystery I am reminded of my own children's conception, the wonder and mystery of it. I am reminded of the angel's message and that God speaks to me as well. I am reminded that there was a time, too, when I was but a spark of life in my mother's womb, a child of God. It is a source of great joy.

> *Mary said, "Here am I, the servant of the Lord; let it be with me according to your word." Then the angel departed from her.—Luke 1:38*

SECOND JOYFUL MYSTERY
The Visitation

Mary set out and went with haste to a Judean town in the hill country, where she entered the house of Zechariah and greeted Elizabeth. When Elizabeth heard Mary's greeting, the child leaped in her womb.—Luke 1:39–41

Two women, fat with babies inside, bumping bellies as they hug. What a wonderful image of friendship between two women! What is more intimate than two pregnant women visiting together, sharing their pregnancies? Mary, a teenager, and Elizabeth, an older woman, yet both bearing their first child. Without denying or taking away from the love and friendship that can arise between a man and a woman, there is something very special about friendships between women.

In her pregnancy, whom does Mary turn to but another woman? Was this the equivalent of sending Mary away in shame to have her baby somewhere she wouldn't be known, as has been done in the past to unwed mothers? Was this meant as a "cooling off" time for Joseph, allowing him to sort things out, figure out what to do? I don't know. What I do know is that this appears to me as a wonderful tribute to friendship. The only other friendship in Scripture that compares is that of Ruth and Naomi. Once again it is a friendship between an older woman and a younger woman, although the relationship between Ruth and Naomi strikes me as one of mentoring, whereas for Mary and Elizabeth it is more one of equals meeting despite age

13

differences. After all, it is the first pregnancy for both women. They are sharing together a very special experience, whereas Naomi acted as a guide to Ruth, helping Ruth from her years of experience.

Mary and Elizabeth remind me of my own female friends. How important they are to me. How much they have meant to me. How they have helped me through difficult times just by their presence and willingness to listen without judgment. They understand me in ways the men in my life have never been able to. It's an understanding that goes beyond words. With men I always have to explain and yet they still often don't get it. With my female friends no explanation is necessary.

But, even more, we have within this friendship the seed of another friendship, that between Jesus and John the Baptist, two babies, two cousins and two great men. I can't help but think they must have been friends growing up. We know so little about Zechariah and Elizabeth, but we do know they were old when John was born. Chances are that they both died before John began his active adult ministry. Besides being cousins, Jesus and John shared the experience of losing their fathers. Perhaps they had played together, comforted each other in their losses in the way that men friends comfort each other. As adults there was no sign between Jesus and John of the competition that so often marks male friendships. There was a competition among their followers but not between themselves. There was a relationship of mutual respect and admiration, a mature male friendship, as mysterious to me in its differences from female friendship as female friendships are to men.

Relationships are truly one of God's great mysteries, as the mystery of one individual interacts with the mystery of another individual. This second mystery is a celebration of life and friendships, friendships that cross generations as well as those among peers, male bonding and female bonding. Friendships continue to be one of life's greatest gifts as well as a mystery!

> *My soul magnifies the Lord,*
> *and my spirit rejoices in God my Savior,*
> *for he has looked with favor on the*
> *lowliness of his servant.*
> *Surely, from now on all generations will*
> *call me blessed.—Luke 1:47–48*

THIRD JOYFUL MYSTERY
The Birth of Jesus

While they were there, the time came for her to deliver her child. And she gave birth to her firstborn son and wrapped him in bands of cloth, and laid him in a manger, because there was no place for them in the inn.
—Luke 2:6–7

A baby born, lying in a manger. How much was Mary able to appreciate the events around this miraculous birth? Certainly her focus wasn't so much on her surroundings or the many visitors, angelic and otherwise, but rather on the birth process itself. It had not been the ideal situation, first traveling so far, having no place to go, giving birth so far away from her parents. She had wanted to be at home, in Nazareth, with her mother close at hand when she gave birth. Instead, here she was in this stable with only Joseph to assist her.

I see Mary as tired from the journey and ready to tell the angelic choir to quiet down and let her sleep, ready to turn away the shepherds. But that would take too much energy, so she smiled and put up with the inconvenience, hoping Joseph would finally politely shoo everyone away. But what of Joseph? He was excited by the events of the night and anxious to talk. He watched in amazement while the angels sang and chatted with the shepherds, until he finally noticed that Mary wanted quiet and sent them away.

Certainly Mary would need the strength that came out of childbirth when dealing with the other trials of motherhood. It would have been only in retrospect that she could reflect on the marvelous events of that night and wonder.

The birth of a child is a truly wonderful event, especially in retrospect. I didn't think too much about the wonder of what was happening with the birth of my children at the actual time of the event, especially with the birth of my firstborn, who arrived in his own time after over thirty hours of labor and a painful episiotomy. Or with the births of my daughters, who came, one in a hurry, hardly giving me time to make it to the delivery room, and the other, two and a half hours later. Some things are much better in the remembering.

This is the mystery of birth. Each time I pray the joyful mysteries, I look forward to this one because each time I pray it I am reminded, not just of Jesus' birth, but of the birth of each of my children. Certainly not the momentous event for the world that Jesus' birth was, but momentous for me. Everything else in my life pales in comparison. There were no angels singing or bright stars lighting up the sky, and yet for me there could easily have been all of this and more. I just couldn't notice in the pain of the moment. Looking back, it's as if the events are filled with a holy light as God gave me this great gift, my children. The struggles and trials of the years don't take that away, but rather enhance it.

Mary, what did you think of that baby, that gift from God, born in less than favorable circumstances? For you, there were actual angels and singing. I wonder if there are angels and singing each time a child is born, and it's just that we here, mired in this world, do not have ears to hear it! But the birth of your son was such a momentous event, not just for you but for the whole world, that the veil between heaven and earth opened momentarily so that we might get a taste of God's glory.

Mary, you were no stranger to angelic visitors, both you and Joseph. You were accustomed to their presence. No wonder the sky filled with their song at the birth of your son. Wonder, Counselor, Prince of Peace, Almighty God—awfully big titles for such a little baby, for such tiny shoulders to bear. Your shoulders were not made to carry such burdens, Jesus. Let me carry them for you as your mother did before me. Let me hold you close, protect you from all harm and love you. How can our God, who is unlimited, fit into such a small container so that such as I may hold you? It is a wonder to me! Our God who wraps us in his mighty arms, holds us in the palm of his hands, lying vulnerable in our human arms. Allowing himself to be powerless and vulnerable so that we might freely choose to love him, not out of fear, but in return for the love he gave us, a tender, caring love. Who am I to hold such a child in my arms? Who are any of us that God should come to us in the form of a baby? What a wonderful image! What a wonderful mystery! Our God, creator of the universe, who knew us in our mother's womb and wraps us in loving arms, allows us to touch him, hold him and cradle him in our arms!

> *So they went with haste and found Mary and Joseph, and the child lying in the manger. When they saw this, they made known what had been told them about this child; and all who heard it were amazed at what the shepherds told them. But Mary treasured all these words and pondered them in her heart.*
> *—Luke 2:16–19*

FOURTH JOYFUL MYSTERY

The Presentation

> *Now there was a man in Jerusalem whose name was Simeon; this man was righteous and devout, looking forward to the consolation of Israel, and the Holy Spirit rested on him. . . . There was also a prophet, Anna the daughter of Phanuel, of the tribe of Asher. She was of a great age, having lived with her husband seven years after her marriage, then as a widow to the age of eighty-four. She never left the temple but worshipped there with fasting and prayer night and day.*
> *—Luke 2:25; 36–37*

An old man and an old woman, living out their lives, good lives of prayer and service, waiting for the fulfillment of a promise. Anna, the prophetess; Simeon, the man who had been promised he would not die before seeing the savior. Quite the pair!

Finally, they see a young couple, simple, poor people, bringing in their firstborn son. The spirit spoke to them, urged them, told them, this was the one, the one for whom they had been waiting. Now they may die in peace. A beginning and an ending. A baby and an older couple. One newly come from God; the others, soon to go to God. Funny how the two extremes of life are so close as life comes full circle. How often that happens. One is born; another dies.

But in this situation there is so much more going on. The one who had recently come from God, also is God. He is the fulfillment of a promise. A promise to a people made so long ago, the promise of a savior, the Messiah. Also a promise to this man, Simeon. Jesus is a promise fulfilled. Quite a lot for a small baby, but, of course, this was no ordinary baby.

Babies are full of promise. They are all potential. We know not what they are to become. Simeon and Anna in their old age are promises fulfilled. Their lives have been lived. It is no longer a matter of wondering what they will become but of reflecting on all that has been, all that has made them who they are.

Jesus, the baby, is both promise of things to come and promise fulfilled. He is the fulfillment of the promise of a Messiah, yet how he will live out this promise is yet to be known. His parents dutifully take him to the temple. What is he to become? They don't know. It remains a mystery. He is a great gift and a great mystery. He came from God and he is brought to God, rightfully so, to the temple, out of obedience. How often will they take him to the temple, carrying him when he is too small to walk, taking him by the hand and leading his little legs until he is old enough to go on his own?

I, too, have carried babies to the "temple" to be baptized. I have led small hands and little feet and dragged reluctant adolescent feet till old enough to go on their own. Will all of this pay off for me? Did it pay for Mary and Joseph? Jesus was both dutiful Jew and troublemaker, turning over tables and scandalizing religious leaders. If Jesus did no less, perhaps I shouldn't worry as my maturing children challenge hypocrisy they see in the church or question beliefs I hold dear.

Mary and Joseph had no way of knowing at the time what the future would hold for their child. As dutiful devout Jews they brought Jesus to the temple. They were faithful to the tradition, did their best to instill a faith in this child and the rest was up to God and the child. In the same way, I do the best I can. I take my children to church and hope that the seed of faith planted in their baptism will continue to be nurtured and grow. I hope that their promise will be fulfilled.

There have been so many promises in my life. Some have been kept, others haven't. Some have been kept but in a form I would never have expected. Some better than I had ever expected. There have been many dreams in my life. Some have come true, some have been shattered and scattered to the wind. Not all dreams are meant to come true. Amidst this world of shattered dreams and broken promises comes a child, a baby. Jesus is the fulfillment of all our hopes and dreams. Jesus is a promise fulfilled, but not what was expected. He was better than expected. Better than human mind could have conceived. Better than an earthly ruler or powerful king! Jesus comes as a reminder that God always keeps his promises to us.

Our children hold so much promise. We marvel as we watch them develop. They are so much more than we could ever conceive on our own, in our little minds. May they fulfill all the promise that is their life . . . May we fulfill that promise, as well, just as Anna and Simeon did.

> *And the child's father and mother were amazed at what was being said about him. Then Simeon blessed them and said to his mother Mary, "This child is destined for the falling and the rising of many in Israel, and to be a sign that will be opposed so that the inner thoughts of*

many will be revealed—and a sword will pierce your own soul too."—Luke 2:33–35

FIFTH JOYFUL MYSTERY
The Finding in the Temple

> *Now every year his parents went to Jerusalem
> for the festival of the Passover. And when he
> was twelve years old, they went up as usual
> for the festival. When the festival was ended
> and they started to return, the boy Jesus
> stayed behind in Jerusalem, but his parents
> did not know it.—Luke 2:41–43*

A child left behind—not an uncommon occurrence, especially in large families.

"I thought he was with you," says Mary.

"I thought he was with you," replies Joseph.

"Where is he then?" they shout together.

I'm so glad that even the Holy Family had its problems. This small glimpse into their life together shows us that. Somewhere a miscommunication, a misunderstanding. No need to worry in their large extended family. Someone was looking out for him. Besides, he was twelve, almost a man. He did not need constant looking after anymore. So, as in *Home Alone 2: Lost in New York*, Jesus is left behind in the big city of Jerusalem.

There's much there to occupy a young boy's mind, many attractions to catch his eyes, many ways to get into trouble. But Jesus, ever the good child, goes to the place he knows best—the temple. When questioned about why he was there, he astounded all with the words of wisdom coming out of one so young. Who is this boy, Jesus, the Nazarene, the carpenter's son, a mere slip of a boy, almost man? What has he to say to all the learned scholars in the temple? Jesus is at home in his father's house and that is where Mary and Joseph find him. How logical. How sensible. Still, Mary and Joseph are aware of the dangers of the city. They are not ready to let their son go. He is not yet a man. Certainly it is too early. They still have years yet to enjoy his company before he sets out on his own.

What thoughts went through Mary and Joseph's mind on that return trip to Jerusalem? Perhaps Mary fingered her own prayers beads as I finger mine when worried about my children and as my own mother before me fingered hers. Certainly, there was no rest for her. Who could sleep when a child was missing?

Memories of all those years went through their heads. The wonder of their firstborn's birth. The angels. The dangerous journey to Egypt. Perhaps Joseph thought about how he had taken his young family on that long journey to Egypt in order to protect his son's young life. Joseph, father and protector. Had he saved his son back then only to lose him now, still so young? Perhaps he had failed as a father in his responsibility to protect this child of his.

What parents are ever truly ready to let go of their children? Certainly not when they are only twelve years old. Maybe by the time they are eighteen or twenty, but not at twelve. We aren't then ready to let go. It's too soon. And yet our children are all too ready to remind us that let go we must. If not today, then soon. We can't keep them babies forever.

A comedy of errors. A series of miscommunications that could have ended in a tragedy, but tragedy was averted. How many times in my own family have there been misunderstandings and miscommunication? Concern is mistaken by teen minds for overprotection, criticism and control. We think we've made ourselves clear, only to find what we thought we had communicated was not what was heard. It seems to be an inevitable part of family life, especially in the teen years. The only way to deal with it? With patience, trust, love, a willingness to admit our mistakes, a willingness to start over.

Mary in anger and concern chastises Jesus. Jesus calmly replies, "Don't you know me by now, mother? Don't you see you had nothing to fear? I'm a responsible, level-headed kid. Certainly, I wasn't out partying all night. I went to the temple where I knew I would be safe and you would find me. Now let's go home and say no more about this." Role reversal—the boy Jesus becomes the adult, calming his parents' fears. They go home together and no more is said about this. They take up where they had left off, but Mary ponders this in her heart, "My little boy is growing up!"

So ends the joyful mysteries. Those joyful years of childhood when we can still maintain some semblance of control, even though it is an illusion. The child is growing up and can no longer be protected. He has to be allowed to be who he was meant to be. After all, it is for this that he was born. Still it is hard, that bridge between childhood and adulthood. Our children are with us for such a short time. They grow up way too soon, despite how it may seem when they are little. Those years pass, oh so quickly. Soon we are left with wonderful memories to treasure all the remainder of our life.

Then he went down with them and came to Nazareth, and was obedient to them. His mother treasured all these things in her heart.—Luke 2:51

A Prayerful Pause
From the Joyful Mysteries to the Mysteries of Light

So much time passes between that last joyful mystery and the beginning of the sorrowful mysteries. Jesus goes from twelve years old to thirty-three—twenty-one years. Mary is no longer a young wife and mother, but a mature woman, well into mid-life by our standards, a matriarch in her time. So much is left out. Should there be another five decades of the rosary to cover the years of Jesus' ministry? Perhaps they could be called the ordinary mysteries and deal with all of the wonderful mysteries of daily life and ministry. The heartaches and the joys, the excitement of following a great leader, feeling you are part of something greater than yourself, and the boredom and tiredness of daily life—getting up and doing the same thing over and over again without seeming to make any progress. Certainly there would be merit in this. Certainly I could use that when feeling tired and discouraged.

If I were to choose these ordinary mysteries, I would start with the wedding at Cana as a celebration of married life. As much as a marriage is a special celebration for those getting married and their families and friends, it's still very much a part of ordinary life. We are born, grow up, marry, have children of our own and die. Despite the growing number of single adults in our society, being married is still very much the norm. Why not celebrate this special event of ordinary life with its own mystery? Marriage is a great mystery both to those married and those outside looking in. What is it that brings these particular individuals together? Why is it that some marriages that seem to be made in heaven fail after a few years, whereas others that you never thought would make it last a lifetime? What does she see in him? What does he see in her? You take two unique individuals and together they form a partnership that is greater than the sum total of the two. You form a marriage as unique as the individuals involved. For all our efforts to study married life it still remains a mystery to most of us.

Then I would have a mystery for Jesus' healing ministry, but which to choose? Perhaps the healing of the man born blind, or the paralytic, or the woman with hemorrhage. Which one would best represent this important aspect of Jesus' ministry? We could easily have five decades dedicated to Jesus' healing ministry and call them the healing mysteries.

And one for Jesus' teaching ministry. This was another important aspect of Jesus' daily ministry. Perhaps the Sermon on the Mount. This includes so many beautiful instructions from Jesus, such as the command to love our enemies and return good for evil. And one for Jesus' ministry of forgiveness of sin. For this I would choose the woman caught in adultery. What a beautiful example, not only of forgiveness, but of how Jesus turned the tables on people so that this woman's accusers had to look at themselves. And what about Jesus casting out demons? Another important aspect of Jesus' ministry. And raising Lazarus from the dead? Or one to celebrate Jesus' compassion for others—"Jesus wept." Or one about Jesus at prayer? And what about the parables? My choices would be the Forgiving

Father/Prodigal Son. So many to choose from. I'd need at least twenty mysteries. Perhaps that is why in the past the church chose not to focus on this aspect of Jesus' life in designating the mysteries. There are just too many to choose from. Or perhaps it was because Mary is not featured in her son's ministry, which doesn't mean she wasn't there as one of Jesus' followers.

Why we only had three sets of mysteries was a mystery to me. Into this mystery comes our pope with the mysteries of light that he announced in the fall of 2002. It took someone with more wisdom than I to choose just five from the many possible choices. In these mysteries we see Jesus the adult in his years of ministry. We see him at his best, instituting the sacraments of baptism, marriage and Eucharist. We see him transformed before our eyes and preaching God's kingdom. Through reflecting on these mysteries we grow in our knowledge of this person, who was both God and man.

THE MYSTERIES
OF LIGHT

FIRST MYSTERY OF LIGHT
The Baptism of Jesus

"You are my Son, the Beloved; with you I am well pleased."—Luke 3:22

What child wouldn't love to hear such words from their parent? Such simple words, but possessing such an impact. Some adults spend their lives seeking the approval from their parents that they never received as children—words of praise sincerely spoken by a parent. Sometimes it takes so little and can mean so much. Certainly this was a source of great strength to Jesus, enabling him to do many things. Without this affirmation, would he have had the courage to confront the hypocrisy of the Pharisees, to boldly chase demons out of those possessed, heal the sick and forgive sins?

In Luke's Gospel these words are spoken directly to Jesus; in Matthew's Gospel they are spoken for the benefit of the crowd. In one instance they are words of affirmation spoken to Jesus; in the other they are spoken about Jesus to let us know who this man is. Later, in the Transfiguration we are told to listen to Jesus in a passage that parallels that of Jesus' baptism. It is a call for all of us to recognize who this man is and to follow him.

Certainly, Jesus was God, but the question remains as to how and when he became aware of this. Was it from birth, or was the awareness developed over time? Just as small children are not able fully to grasp concepts adults can grasp, perhaps as a child Jesus' ability to grasp his identity was limited by his human form. Just as children's identity develops slowly over time and needs affirmation from significant people around them, perhaps Jesus' sense of identity developed over time to finally be confirmed with his baptism and these words from his Father. Regardless of how and when Jesus came to realize his identity, his relationship with his heavenly Father was a close one, a source of strength throughout his adult life.

Words of affirmation spoken by a parent are important for a child's developing sense of self-worth and identity. How much more powerful when spoken by our God. These words spoken to Jesus are also spoken to each one of us. We are children of God and, as such, are beloved. In times of trials when I am discouraged and wonder whether or not what I am doing makes a difference, these words are a source of comfort to me. They give me the strength to go on in the face of seemingly insurmountable obstacles. The knowledge that our heavenly Father is proud of me keeps me going. Without it I would never be able to live up to the challenge posed by our baptism—the challenge of following in the footsteps of Jesus.

> *"This is my Son, the Beloved, with whom
> I am well pleased."—Matthew 3:17*

SECOND MYSTERY OF LIGHT
The Wedding at Cana

> *Jesus did this, the first of his signs, in Cana*
> *of Galilee, and revealed his glory; and his dis-*
> *ciples believed in him.—John 2:11*

How remarkable that Jesus should perform his first miracle at a wedding, and at the request of his mother, no less. Perhaps he had much bigger ideas. Perhaps he had wanted his first miracle to be truly spectacular, right up there with Moses' parting of the Red Sea. Perhaps the idea of changing water into wine at a wedding had seemed rather trivial and unimportant in light of all the other needs pressing for his attention. I know it probably would have seemed so to me. Why waste a miracle on a party? Wouldn't it be better used to cast out a demon or raise someone from the dead? And yet, performing a miracle at a wedding party is precisely what Jesus did, out of respect for his mother, and we continue to reap the benefits of his action.

In a world where marriages are often under attack and where as many as half of all marriages end in divorce, Jesus reaffirms the importance of marriage by his actions. He raises to the level of a sacrament this civil union. He reaffirms the importance of the fourth commandment, as well, in his respect for his mother, honoring her request above his own wishes. He affirms the importance of celebrating these significant moments in our lives. In our American society, a society of workaholics with increasingly less leisure time, everything doesn't always have to be about work. Sometimes God's will is that we celebrate with family and friends and give praise to God through our celebrations.

This miracle is also a reminder that God works in many ways. What may seem insignificant to us may prove to be the most important thing we do in this life. What may have seemed like an insignificant act on the part of Jesus has taken on greater significance over time and continues to be a source of reflection for future generations.

Jesus was obedient to his mother in honoring her request and the waiters were obedient in doing what Jesus told them. In the same way we need to be obedient in response to what God asks of us, regardless of how seemingly insignificant.

> *His mother said to the servants, "Do whatever he tells you." —John 2:5*

THIRD MYSTERY OF LIGHT
The Proclamation of the Kingdom and the Call to Conversion

*"Let us go on to the neighboring towns, so that
I may proclaim the message there also; for
that is what I came out to do."—Mark 1:38*

Jesus in Mark's Gospel is a man on the move. He is a
man of action. He has a mission and wastes no time in
setting about accomplishing this mission. In the course
of the first chapter, Jesus is baptized, tempted in the
desert, calls his first disciples and performs many miracles, including curing a demoniac, a leper, Peter's
mother-in-law and many others. To read this chapter in
one sitting is enough to leave you breathless. Of course,
three years is a relatively short time to do something.
No wonder he was in such a hurry. He had no time to
waste in proclaiming the Good News of God's kingdom.
But what about us, those of us living today? Certainly
we cannot keep up the pace that Jesus set. Paul was
similar to Mark's Jesus in his sense of mission and
urgency to spread the Good News. How do we preach the
gospel in our day and age? We, who are not anticipating
the imminent arrival of the Parousia. We, who have
family concerns that take up our time. We, too, are
called to preach the gospel. How do we do it?

There are days when I wonder, have I somehow gone
astray? Have I lost the idealism of my youth when it
comes to following Jesus? Sometimes it feels like it is all
I can do just to stay afloat. There are bills to pay, tuition

checks for Catholic schools, home repairs, car repairs. There are many things that need to be maintained in a home. There are doctor bills, orthodontist bills, bills for glasses, dentist bills. Then there's food and clothing to buy, meals to prepare, dishes to wash, laundry to do. Some days I feel that all I am doing is surviving, much less preaching God's word.

But Jesus only had three years, I have a whole lifetime to be faithful to God's word and preach it with my life. The time and energy I put into my home and into my children is not time wasted, but time put to good use in that they, too, need to learn to love God and serve him.

I can't keep up the pace that Jesus sets, but I don't have to do that. I have many more years to love and serve God while on this earth. In that my heart is turned to God and I sincerely seek to do his will, I can feel confident that in some small way I, too, am doing my part to bring about God's kingdom. I need a lifetime to do just a small portion of what Jesus did in three years. But that's okay. God will supply the rest.

> *"The kingdom of God is as if someone would scatter seed on the ground, and would sleep and rise night and day, and the seed would sprout and grow, he does not know how. The earth produces of itself, first the stalk, then the head, then the full grain in the head." —Mark 4:26–28*

FOURTH MYSTERY OF LIGHT
The Transfiguration

*Six days later, Jesus took with him Peter and
James and his brother John and led them up
a high mountain, by themselves. And he was
transfigured before them, and his face shone
like the sun, and his clothes became dazzling
white.—Matthew 17:1–2*

There are times when our children are transfigured
before our eyes. When they are cleaned up, in their
Sunday best and singing in the children's choir at
church. Or when performing at a recital, or when you
catch them unaware showing maturity beyond their
years in speaking to a friend or performing an act of
service. These are the moments for which parents live!
They are glimpses of the adults our children could be,
glimpses of them at their best. Yes, these glimpses are
rare and short-lived as these same children quickly
destroy any lingering illusions we may have about them
by running through the school halls or fighting with
their brothers or sisters. Still, these moments are all the
more precious for being so few and far between. It's
almost as if our children want to let us know—don't get
any funny ideas about me being like this all the time!
They don't want to get caught doing a good deed because
of the expectation that it might raise in us. They don't
want us to pitch a tent and expect them to continue to
act that way any more than Jesus would let Peter pitch
a tent.

Peter, James and John catch but a glimpse of Jesus' glory, but it was enough for Peter right away to want to set up camp and remain there—one of the great dangers of such mountaintop experiences. So often when they occur we want to hold on to them when we can't. We have to come down from the mountain. Jesus wisely brings them back down and instructs them to tell no one, lest they get some funny ideas about him and try to make him king. Our children bring us back down to earth, at times quite rudely, lest we get any funny notions about who they are meant to be, rather than allowing them to work out their own salvation with fear and trembling over time. They don't want to be locked into our expectations of them any more than Jesus will allow us to lock him into any box of false expectations, any more than any of us want to be locked into other's expectations of us.

So, we all must come down from the mountain in good time. But while those moments last, enjoy them for what they are—just glimpses of the glory that awaits for those who love God.

> *Then Peter said to Jesus, "Lord, it is good for us to be here."—Matthew 17:4*

FIFTH MYSTERY OF LIGHT
The Institution
of the Eucharist

Then Jesus took the loaves, and when he had
given thanks, he distributed them to those
who were seated.—John 6:11

When I meet with parents preparing for their child's
first Eucharist, I like to do a simple exercise. First, I ask
the parents to think back to their own first communions
and to write on a sheet of paper the first thing that
comes to mind. Then I ask them to share their responses
with others. Usually there is a lot of laughter as the parents recall the clothing they wore, the gifts received and
parties held. Then I ask them to think about their experience of Eucharist now, as an adult, and to write what
comes to mind. This is much harder, as people struggle
to find the words to express what Eucharist means to
them today. They come up with much more abstract concepts: peace, joy, the Body of Christ, humility that God
would come to them. It's a very simple exercise and yet
it brings home to them both where their children are in
their understanding and how their understanding
changes over time. It's also good for them to take a
minute to reflect on the place of the Eucharist in their
lives, something we often have little time for in all our
busyness.

I pray each time that I am involved in preparing
young children for receiving Jesus in the Eucharist that
through this time of preparation not only will their parents grow in their understanding of this great mystery,

but that I will as well. It is a powerful prayer—one that challenges me greatly.

If we truly believe what we say about the Eucharist, that it is the very body of Christ, then our churches should be packed every Sunday. Not only on Sunday, but each day of the week as well. What is it that keeps us from doing this? Many of our Protestant brothers and sisters don't celebrate communion each week. It is reserved for special occasions, lest in receiving too often communion become commonplace and lose its special-ness. I can appreciate this line of reasoning, but I have to wonder: if Jesus had wanted us to reserve the cele-bration of communion to just special occasions, then why did he use such a common substance as bread? Why not something more festive, such as cake? But Jesus chose bread, a basic staple of life that we might come to know him and grow closer to him. Jesus, too, wants to be a basic staple of our lives, as necessary as the food we eat.

Each time we pray the Lord's Prayer, we say, "give us this day our daily bread." In the same way Jesus wants to come to us each day. Why do we hold back? Lack of time? The inconvenience of fitting a Mass time into our busy schedule? I certainly know these excuses very well for I use them myself.

Still I pray to grow in understanding and apprecia-tion for this great mystery of our faith in which Jesus comes to us in the form of simple bread and wine, basic staples of life and basic staples of our faith.

> *"I am the bread of life. Whoever comes to me will never be hungry, and whoever believes in me will never be thirsty."*
> —*John 6:35*

A PRAYERFUL PAUSE
From the Mysteries of Light to the Sorrowful Mysteries

All that Jesus does during his years of active ministry leads inevitably to this: his suffering and death. Jesus, like all of us, had choices to make. Had he not made the choices he made as an adult, perhaps the outcome would have been different. Perhaps if he had been more careful in his challenging of religious authorities, perhaps if he had softened his rhetoric and been more politically correct, he could have avoided this death. Perhaps, but perhaps not. We can spin wheels second-guessing choices, but once the choices are made we can't go back. Each of the choices we make in our life sets us on a path. We can alter that path by future choices but we can't change the past. In that we make these choices with God in mind, chances are we won't go too far astray from where God wants us to go. We may make mistakes, but God can take care of those mistakes as long as we let him.

Jesus sets his face to Jerusalem throughout the three years of his active ministry. Each action he took, each choice he made, brought him closer to his death. In the same way each action we take, each choice we make will lead us to some future, and eventually to our own death. We can maybe postpone this but we can't avoid it. Jesus' death was not the result of mistaken judgments on his part but the result of a life well lived, a life of service to God.

Jesus, the little baby in the joyful mysteries, so full of promise, grows up and completes that promise in his suffering and death. In reflecting on these mysteries we find comfort and strength for all who are sorrowing and struggling under life's burdens. In a world obsessed with being happy and the pursuit of happiness as a birth-right, it's a comfort to have these mysteries as a reminder that suffering is also a part of living. It's right and appropriate to grieve when dealing with the harder aspects of this life. And so let us join Mary as we reflect on the last day of her son's life on this earth.

THE SORROWFUL
MYSTERIES

FIRST SORROWFUL MYSTERY
The Agony in the Garden

He came out and went, as was his custom, to the Mount of Olives; and the disciples followed him.—Luke 22:39

Staying up all night before a big day, waiting up, praying non-stop—I know what that is. I'm no stranger to long nights. There are plenty of reasons to keep a parent awake. Staying up with sick children, walking the floor with colicky babies, waiting up for children coming home from a late date or the prom, tossing and turning the night before the wedding, waiting to hear about the new arrival, staying up in hospital rooms keeping vigil. The apostles fell asleep, but I bet Mary didn't. How could a parent sleep knowing her son was troubled? How could she sleep for her worry?

Jesus knew what was ahead of him. Did Mary have even a clue? Maybe. She must have sensed something. She was around till the end, at the foot of the cross. She didn't just happen to be there by chance. Chances are she was around the night before. It's not like she could jet in from Nazareth for the day. She had to have been close by. She had to have known her son was upset.

She wasn't invited to stay awake with him. Maybe Jesus sent her home, wanting to spare her his turmoil, wanting her to get a good night's sleep. Lie down she might have, but sleep . . . only fitfully. As much as Jesus may have tried to spare her, he couldn't, any more than Mary could have spared him. She went back to the house where she was staying with Mary Magdalene and the other women in order to ease his mind, but stay up she must have. Jesus did not keep vigil alone. Mary was awake as any parent would be. As fervently as Jesus prayed that this cup might pass him by, Mary prayed just as fervently for her son's safety. "Take me instead," she pleaded. "I'm old. I've outlived my use. Take me, not him, not my son. He's all I have left since Joseph died. Please take me, not him."

She prayed and prayed, cried, pleaded until she, too, found some rest, some peace, the ability to accept whatever would happen. How else could she have managed to last through the crucifixion if she had not been fortified by the power of prayer? Just as Jesus' vigil prepared him for what lay ahead, Mary's vigil prepared her. As hard as it was for Jesus, it was also hard for Mary. How was she going to make it through this?

Which is harder to do? To ride forth, ready to do battle, ready to die, or to remain behind, pick up the pieces, support our children in their undertakings even when we don't understand them? Did Mary try to talk Jesus out of what he was doing? Did she try to talk him into leaving Jerusalem, finding a safe haven? Maybe that's why she wasn't invited to the garden with Jesus. Maybe she was like Peter in trying to protect Jesus from what was to come, so Jesus said, "Get behind me, Satan." Maybe. What parent wouldn't do whatever necessary to save their child? But in the end, she, too, was compliant with God's will. As hard as it was, she, too, had to say, "your will, not mine."

Mary had her own agony in the garden. We share in this agony whenever we wrestle with God, whenever we struggle to accept God's will in our lives. When we question, fight, resist and finally give in, even though we don't fully understand the reason why. There have been events in my life that I have struggled over. Some have taken years of my life to resolve and come to some sense of peace. I have struggled with wanting to do God's will but wondering what that was. Did Mary question that it was God's will that her son die? I certainly would have questioned it. He was to be the messiah, the savior. How was he to save his people from a cross? How could he save them once dead? It's hard enough to accept God's will if you know that it is God's will, but when you don't know—that's the agony of it.

I have struggled for years trying to discern God's will, wondering if I've got it right or am only deluding myself. This agony has been much longer than one intense night, but many nights. Despite this struggle to discern, God's will remains a mystery to me. That's part of the agony and the ecstasy of being human, being a parent. There were probably many nights when Mary lay awake wondering and worrying about her son. Wondering— had she gotten it wrong? Had she been a good enough mother? Had she taught him well enough, or had she failed in this most important job? She wondered and worried even while her son slept peacefully, wandering through Galilee. She wondered and worried as she saw her son take steps that she knew may very well lead to this day. She wondered and worried because, after all, she was a parent. That's what we parents do.

> *"I am deeply grieved, even to death;*
> *remain here, and stay awake with me."*
> —*Matthew 26:38*

SECOND SORROWFUL MYSTERY
The Scourging at the Pillar

Now the men who were holding Jesus began to mock him and beat him; they also blindfolded him and kept asking him, "Prophesy! Who is it that struck you?" They kept heaping many other insults on him.—Luke 22:63–65

"Sticks and stones may break my bones but names will never hurt me." Who hasn't heard this at one time or another? As parents we tell our children this to toughen them up, to prepare them for the slings and arrows of unkind words that await them on the schoolyard and in the world. Yet we know the lie of this statement. Name-calling, unkind, hurtful words, gossip, slander are very much like sticks and stones thrown against us, tearing our skin, seeking out the tender spots and lacerating them like the lashes of the cat-o'-nine-tails used to scourge Jesus. Children can be incredibly cruel and insensitive on the playground, in the lunchroom, in the locker room. This has been brought to the forefront of our national attention by the incident at Columbine, in which teens who had apparently been outcasts, teased and bullied, in an act of insanity picked up rifles and shot their classmates and teacher. Teasing and bullying have always been with us, but are they part of a harmless rite of passage or destructive of individuals? As parents we watch in anguish and hope our children will hold up under this assault.

Gossip is like lashes, tearing at the soul, leaving marks that don't easily heal. We are helpless under the attack. We don't see our attackers but we feel their sting, just as Jesus was unable to see his assailants. We helplessly watch as others try to hold up under their attack but our hands are tied like Jesus'. We can't turn and confront our assailants for they hide in anonymity.

Gossip and slander are terrible vices. It's awful to be their victim. It's equally awful to see those you love under their attack. You want to protect your loved one, stop the abuse, but your hands are tied as well. Words said in support can be twisted and used against your loved one, making the situation even worse rather than better. We stagger under the blows or cringe as we watch helplessly.

I don't know what it is to be scourged as Jesus was, but I do know what it is to be scourged by words and to watch as loved ones are scourged. I've dried tears of my own children and other children hurt by unkind words of classmates. In this day and age we do not punish and humiliate with forty lashes, but with verbal lashes.

How Mary must have longed to pour healing salve or ointment on those wounds, to hold her son and reassure him that all would be okay, to kiss away the pain like we kissed the boo-boos of childhood, but she could not. As my children grow older, the hurts seem to cut deeper: broken friendships, betrayal, the heartbreak of breaking up, lost jobs, lost honors they had worked for and hoped for. They don't kill, but they hurt. They cut deep.

Each time we gossip, each time we utter untruths, unkindnesses against others, we are lashing Jesus again. Each time we allow this to go on we are participating in the scourging. There are thousands of ways in which we scourge Jesus daily, not just with words, but with kindness not done, wrongs left uncorrected. These are not death blows, but many little cuts, lacerations that weaken us and make it harder to go on. Under their blows we become discouraged, worn down, we ask, "What's the use?"

The world can be so cruel. There can be worse things than death. The ways we punish and torture each other become more sophisticated with each age, yet they remain cruel and crude weapons whose only purpose is to tear down and destroy. They are the modern cat-o'-nine-tails. How I long to protect my children from all of this, but it is too much, too big, bigger than I am, especially when dealing with a hidden enemy. Like Mary, I watch with anguish as my children venture out into a cruel world. I hope I've done all I can for them, to help them withstand the blows, but I can't always be there for them to protect them. I can't change the whole world, but I can do my best to make the world a better place, a place where it is easier to be good. I can work to make the world a better place for my children, grandchildren and all children.

> *Now the chief priests and the whole council were looking for false testimony against Jesus so that they might put him to death. —Matthew 26:59*

THIRD SORROWFUL MYSTERY
Jesus Is Crowned with Thorns

. . . after twisting some thorns into a crown, they put it on his head. They put a reed in his right hand and knelt before him and mocked him, saying, "Hail, King of the Jews!" They spat on him and took the reed and struck him on the head.—Matthew 27:29–30

Talk about a migraine headache. My head throbs just thinking about it, and I have had my share of headaches. I know of the throbbing, pounding pain, sometimes sharp and forceful, other times low, nagging, hidden below the surface, never quite going away. The one is debilitating. Nothing can be done. No one can think clearly to act when suffering its pain. The other is just there, ever present, nagging, threatening to become a full-blown head pounder. It clouds your judgment and hinders full functioning, but your ability to function remains.

Jesus, with head pounding, is brought before Pilate. How could Jesus even begin to respond with any coherence? But respond he did. He didn't grovel, despite the pain. Think of all the times that, as a parent, you had to carry on despite being sick or in pain, times you put food on the table despite a pounding headache, times you refereed fighting children even though your head felt it was about to split apart, times you got up from bed, barely recovered yourself from a bout with the flu, to minister to your children's needs. You did it, just as Jesus did, because to do anything else would have been less than who you truly are as a person. You did it because it seemed to be the right thing to do. So we pull ourselves through, put down our own needs when confronted with needs of family. It doesn't mean we never take care of ourselves, but when the occasion arises, we rise to the occasion, just as Jesus did.

Jesus was hit on the head with a reed. A reed is but a lightweight object with which to strike someone on the head but, when combined with the presence of the thorns, it is but another small thing weighing us down. Think of all the pressing details that are part of being a parent, each sometimes like sharp thorns pressing on our brain, causing a dull ache, a small seepage of your life's blood. Certainly it's not the big things that get to us in the end. I can handle a major crisis. It's the little things, day in and day out, never ending, that never seem to go away completely, that are always there demanding attention and robbing us of sleep. Doctor and dentist appointments to set and keep, clothes to have ready. Pick up the dry cleaning, drop one child here, another child there, all without getting angry and losing your cool. The burden of remembering everybody's schedules, likes and dislikes. I could never understand, as a child, why my mother found it so hard to remember I didn't like butter with my peanut butter sandwiches. I would gag at the yellow lumps lying under the peanut butter and wonder why she couldn't do something as simple as keep my lunch straight from my brothers' and sisters'. Now I wonder that she even managed to make the lunches at all, let alone get them right.

These are the things that can get to you over time. These are the things that can drive parents crazy. They are the thorns in a parent's crown of glory. Jesus bore his crown with dignity and so can we. We can wear the crown as if it isn't even there, trusting in God in whom all things are possible. It doesn't remove the irritations and pain, but gives them meaning and so makes them easier to bear. Some day it will be replaced with a crown of glory. Within the crown of thorns are the makings of the crown of glory for all parents. It is the basis upon which the crown of glory is made, built bit by bit by every gray hair we earn raising our children.

> *So Jesus came out, wearing the crown of thorns and the purple robe. Pilate said to them, "Here is the man!" When the chief priests and the police saw him, they shouted, "Crucify him! Crucify him!"*
> —*John 19:5–6*

Fourth Sorrowful Mystery
Jesus Carries His Cross

> *As they led him away, they seized a man,*
> *Simon of Cyrene, who was coming from the*
> *country, and they laid the cross on him, and*
> *made him carry it behind Jesus.—Luke 23:26*

Jesus fell not just once, but three times, weakened by all he had already endured and under the weight of the cross. By then, how many times had Mary had to watch her son fall, from those first tentative steps when he learned to walk, only to come running back to her, till the day those feet took him away from her as he had to be about the Father's work? And now he falls under a heavy burden, too heavy to bear alone. How she must have longed to help him carry the cross, help him back on his feet, wipe away his tears and tell him it would be all right, as she had done so many times when he was little. But she couldn't do it, couldn't get beyond the soldiers holding back the crowd. Much as she might have longed to help, this was a road he had to walk without her. But how she must have worried as she watched her son struggle under his burden. How we worry as we watch our own children struggle under their own particular crosses.

It is so hard for us parents to allow our children to suffer the consequences of their actions. Jesus had been well aware of what the eventual consequences of his actions might be. He had known that the steps he had taken over the past three years might very well lead him to such a place, but that did not deter him, did not hold him back. Now, even if he had second thoughts, it was too late. No changing the past. All he could do was go forward and all she could do was follow.

All those years of letting go, letting him follow where God led him still could not have prepared her for this. He was still her little boy. How could she go on without him? What was her life without first her husband and now her son? How could she go on? And yet she did. Just as Jesus managed to get back up and continue the course before him, she managed to get up and continue the course before her. No turning back.

Sometimes it's all we can do to keep on going. When the end is near it can seem so easy to give up, to collapse under the weight upon us, but instead we keep going. Some days it seems it is all I can do to crawl out of bed, to continue the course in front of me. I feel discouraged and wonder what is the use. Will any of it make a difference? I want to give up. And yet somehow I find the will to go on, to go forward even when there is seemingly little progress, even when I know the ending place is not where I want to go. Still I find the courage to go on. I find the courage to remain a parent under the most difficult of conditions. I stand beside my children no matter how hard it may be, even when they make choices I disagree with or don't understand. I never stop being a parent, even if that leads me through public despair and humiliation.

What of the parents of children who end up in jail? Whose children don't always make the honor role in school? Who publicly fail? Are they any less parents? Mary stood by her son throughout this difficult day. She didn't run away. She didn't wash her hands of him. When the road grew dark, she followed after him, faithful to the last. She stayed with him no matter how hard. There was a tremendous strength and courage in her. Others would have fallen under such a burden. She didn't. Parents can gather strength and courage from her example. No matter the hardship your children's actions put you through, you remain a parent. Children are not divorceable, even when they reject and abandon you— you remain a parent. Even when they fall many times, you stand by them. Despite all your worries, you give your children the freedom to fail, fall and get back up again. This is one of the greatest gifts we can give our children. And yet we weep for ourselves and our children as we watch them struggle.

> *A great number of the people followed him, and among them were women who were beating their breasts and wailing for him. But Jesus turned to them and said, "Daughters of Jerusalem, do not weep for me, but weep for yourselves and for your children." —Luke 23:27–28*

FIFTH SORROWFUL MYSTERY
Jesus Dies on the Cross

> *It was now around noon, and darkness came over the whole land until three in the afternoon, while the sun's light failed; and the curtain of the temple was torn in two. Then Jesus, crying with a loud voice, said ....*
> —Luke 23:44–46

What a dark day. Jesus is taken down from the cross and laid in his mother's lap. This woman who brought him into the world now witnesses his leaving the world. What greater sorrow than this? In this beautiful image is the sum total of a parent's pain—to lose a child. It is hard to imagine anything more painful.

How often do we suffer mini-deaths where our children are concerned? This baby boy, so full of potential, his life has run full course. There are many things he has done, others he didn't. He will not be there to ease the burden of old age for his mother, to brighten her later years with grandchildren. All she has done, all she is is naught. Gone so quickly. As parents we don't live for our children, and yet they are a very special part of who we are. Once a parent, always a parent. She has to take on yet another role. From mother of a baby, to mother of a toddler, to mother of a growing boy, to mother of an adolescent, to mother of a young adult, mother of a rebel, a leader, a healer, a miracle worker ... Now she has to adjust to yet another role, a final role—mother of a dead child. Her son may be dead, but she will always be a mother. It is part of her identity, part of who she is. Without him she feels loss, yet he will always be her son.

The death of a child upsets the ordinary course of life events. It's unnatural. Children are not supposed to die before their parents, and yet it does happen. Mary grieves, not just for her son but for children everywhere, for parents everywhere. Every time they cry out in agony, holding a sick child, looking for a lost child, grieving a dead child, Mary is there with them, eternal mother, sharing their pain. She grieves with the mothers of South America who cry out for their missing children. She grieves with the parents of heroin addicts who are slowly killing themselves. She grieves with those whose children are in jails awaiting death sentences. Just as she tenderly holds the body of her son and weeps, so she holds each of us as we weep tears together, salt water mixing with salt water. She knows our pain and cries with us. We are not alone in our sorrow.

There is no greater loss than that of a child. A child loved into being, cherished throughout his or her growing years. As parents we are truly united in our cares for our children. It is so often suffering that binds us together, but there we can find healing. Mary had little to brag about as she held her dead child. She had only her grief, a grief she shares with all parents.

The pietà symbolizes the dark side of motherhood. You don't have to have experienced the death of a child to be aware of the suffering that is a natural part of being a parent. There are many agonies that parents go through as they watch children take wing, leave their homes, sometimes leave all that we hold dear. There are many agonies as we witness our children growing up, dealing with their own crosses in life. The heartbreak of romance gone awry, feeling like an outcast at school, the pain of divorce, the pain of illness . . . And yet our lives are richer for the experience. Would we have it any other way? Would we have chosen not to be parents if we had known ahead of time the price we would have to pay?

It is only in embracing the darker aspects of life, as Mary embraces her dead son, that we grow to a maturity of faith, a deepening of all that it means to love, the sorrows as well as the joy inherent in that. It is only through death that we find resurrection. Our sorrows link us together as people much more deeply than our joys.

> *Meanwhile, standing near the cross of Jesus [was] his mother .... —John 19:25*

A PRAYERFUL PAUSE
From the Sorrowful Mysteries to the Glorious Mysteries

[T]he tomb was nearby . . . —John 19:42

Jesus is laid in the tomb. He stayed there such a short time, less than three full days, and yet an eternity for his friends who missed him so much. But three days is not a very long time. Certainly it's not enough time to transition from sorrow to glory, is it? There were fifteen years between the last joyful mysteries and the mysteries of light, and three more years before the first sorrowful mystery. But then the joyful mysteries covered an expanse of thirteen years and the mysteries of light three years. The sorrowful mysteries last but a day. Is that how it is meant to be in the scheme of our lives? Sorrow is but a day, and joy is so much longer?

So much is packed into that one day—a whole lifetime. Jesus experiences in one day what it takes a whole lifetime for most of us to experience. Time is so arbitrary and relative. We put measurements on it and try to structure it into equal portions. Sixty seconds in a minute, sixty minutes in an hour, twenty-four hours in a day. Nice and logical, chronological, but time isn't truly like that. Time can't be fit into nice, neat packages. It spills over, has a mind of its own. One day truly can be a lifetime.

In the church we structure each year. Advent—four weeks before Christmas; Lent—forty days before Easter. Nice neat packaging. We structure our liturgical calendar around these different days. Church ministers lead their people through them as if life can be orchestrated to fit a calendar. Yet life isn't like that. It's messy and knows it's own sense of time. The Advent in my soul may not coincide with the church's liturgical calendar. Lent in my spirit may very well take forty years, just as it took forty years of wandering in the desert for the Hebrew nation. Just because the calendar says it's Easter doesn't mean it is Easter in your soul, doesn't mean you have to feel joyful when in your heart you know you are not ready to be joyful. Lent and Easter are not bound by our ordinary sense of time. They are seasons of the soul. The soul knows the right time.

Jesus spent only one full day in the tomb, two nights. That was enough time for him. It was all he required. After all, he was God. But we are mere mortals. Sometimes the spirit requires a longer resting space between the ending of one portion of life and a new beginning. Sometimes we need to rest in the tomb for a while before we are ready for a resurrection in our life. There is nothing wrong with that.

The years of my marital separation and divorce were very much an experience of being on the cross. When I finally felt that God had said, "It is finished," it was a relief to realize it was over and to lay my spirit in the tomb for however long I needed. The tomb is a good place, a resting place between an ending and a beginning. Far too often we rush from an ending to another beginning, hardly allowing even a day of rest, time out between. But me, I like the tomb. You can't live there forever, but it is there for however long you need it. Don't be afraid to find peace, comfort, rest within its walls before venturing out again.

We all need down time, time in the tomb. However long it takes. Stay till God bids you leave, till God says it's time. In God's own time, we will be ready to share in God's glory.

THE GLORIOUS
MYSTERIES

FIRST GLORIOUS MYSTERY
The Resurrection

> *After the sabbath, as the first day of the week*
> *was dawning, Mary Magdalene and the other*
> *Mary went to see the tomb. And suddenly*
> *there was a great earthquake; for an angel of*
> *the Lord, descending from heaven, came and*
> *rolled back the stone and sat on it.*
> —Matthew 28:1–2

What a shock! What disbelief! To see the stone rolled
away and then to meet a man who resembles the one
you love who has been taken away. Mary Magdalene
must have thought she was seeing things. And yet it
truly was Jesus. Sometimes after one we loved dies we
see people who resemble them. For a moment our heart
jumps into our throat as we think it might be them.
Maybe we were wrong! But then we realize we are mistaken. For Mary Magdalene it was just the opposite. She
didn't recognize Jesus at first. It was only after he spoke
to her that her heart jumped into her throat and she
knew it to be him.

Sometimes upon the death of a loved one there is a
strong sense of that person's presence remaining
throughout the funeral, and sometimes for weeks and
months beyond that. I've experienced this myself as well
as heard many beautiful stories of such "resurrection"
experiences. Loved ones come to say good-bye. They
come in our dreams as well as in our waking moments.
And when a truly great spirit moves on, the impact is
felt much further. Several months after Mother Teresa

of Calcutta's death a speaker who had known her came to our parish. We had a sense of this great woman's presence, which had come all of the way from India to the village of Concord, Michigan. Our sense of her presence remained strong for months after her death. Hers was truly a great spirit.

But the resurrection appearances of Jesus were even more than that, were beyond this and so much more real and powerful. Jesus broke the veil of death and came back to let us know there is more to this life than what we see. Thomas touched him. Jesus broke bread with his disciples, walked with them, talked with them. He was as real as the person sitting next to us. His was truly a great spirit!

What joy, what disbelief, what a mixture of emotions for all of the disciples, but even more so for Mary. And yet, I somehow believe she knew. Somehow in her deepest being, she knew it was not over. She knew that this child, whose arrival had been greeted by hosts of angels, would not lightly go into the next world. She somehow knew there had to be more. Mary was used to welcoming angels. Even as her heart broke and she grieved over the death of her son, part of her waited for more, just as she had waited for her son's birth over thirty-three years earlier. Parents have a way of knowing these things.

Hers wasn't necessarily the ecstatic, surprised joy of Mary of Magdala or the apostles, but a quiet, deeper, powerful joy of confirmation. Her son was not dead. He truly lives. After these days of agony in which her nerves were raw and weary she was finally able to collapse into a quiet, peaceful sleep. She knew. She didn't have to see her son to know and believe.

We have no resurrection account of Jesus appearing to Mary and, yet, why would he not? I imagine he appeared to her as well, briefly, just long enough to confirm what she already knew, and then he was gone again, once again about the Father's business, as he had been so many years ago and as he had been throughout his life. The same in death as in life, and yet moreso. We become more ourselves as we age and in our death, if we age with grace, trusting in the Spirit's guidance.

Death, where is your sting? It is gone for those of us who believe. The pain of loss remains. We grieve but the sharpness of not knowing, the emptiness of the tomb, of wondering if all is for nothing is gone. Mary's womb, once empty, is filled with delight as she realizes her son goes on, his ministry goes on even beyond death. Many parents who have lost children have found new hope, new reason for living, through trying to change the world for their children's sake, in their memory. Thus we have Mothers against Drunk Drivers. We have support groups for those who have lost children. We see parents who have lost children to cancer working to fund research to find a cure. These are all ways of bringing new life out of death.

Death is overcome by the Resurrection and we are filled with awe and wonder. My own experiences with death and dying have confirmed what we know deep in our hearts, and this is reason for rejoicing not weeping.

> *Jesus said to her, "Woman, why are you*
> *weeping? Whom are you looking for?"*
> *—John 20:15*

Second Glorious Mystery
The Ascension into Heaven

> *"But you will receive power when the Holy Spirit has come upon you; and you will be my witnesses in Jerusalem, in all Judea and Samaria, and to the ends of the earth." When he had said this, as they were watching, he was lifted up, and a cloud took him out of their sight.—Acts 1:8–9*

There is no mention of tears or sadness as Jesus leaves this world. And yet this is the final good-bye. They will not see him anymore. Perhaps his disciples didn't believe this, couldn't accept it after the events of the previous five weeks. Our God is a God of surprises. What a surprise it had been when Jesus had showed up after his death. Wouldn't he surprise them once again? Perhaps they couldn't accept that this would truly be the last time they saw him. Denial. Despite what he had told them, he would be back. Who was this spirit, this comforter, he spoke of? They didn't know. So they said their good-byes and went back to the upper room to pray and wait till they knew what to do next.

Often after a loved one has died there is another death that occurs, sometimes a year after the original death. After a year of intense grief and the ups and downs of remembering, thinking about the loved one each moment of the day, sensing their presence even though they are gone, there comes a time when you are finally able to get through part of the day without thinking about your loved one. Their face is no longer constantly before you. You are starting to move on with your life and you panic. You are hit with guilt, over-whelming guilt. How could you stop thinking about this person? How could you move on with your life? How can you experience any joy or happiness knowing he or she is gone? Didn't you love this person? It is the second death and is followed by more of the intense grieving that followed the early months of your loss. You could go on as long as you held those memories close, thought about your loved one every day and sensed their pres-ence in your life, but now that is slipping away from you and you panic and grieve.

Jesus assures his friends that he will not leave them alone. He will send a comforter. Jesus doesn't want us to hang on to him physically, nor does he want us to hang on to our grief. We need to let him go, as we need to let our loved ones go. Honoring their memory doesn't mean holding onto the grief but rather letting go and trusting in what may come next.

What parent can ever forget a child? Anniversaries of birthdays and the anniversary of the moment of death are painful reminders of all we have lost. This second death must have been every bit as painful to Mary as the first. This was the final letting go. God may have given her special grace to bear God's son through all she had to bear, but that didn't spare her feeling every bit of the grief, every ounce of the feelings associated with being a mother. God's grace helped her bear up under the unbearable but it didn't free her from experiencing every bit, every ounce of life. If anything, it helped her experience life to the fullest, with sharp pain, piercing joy and radiating peace. Mary was free from sin but every bit human, every bit a parent who suffered the full range of emotions of parenthood. This is what makes the glorious mysteries glorious. Not that Mary was given the grace to escape the pains of this life but that she experienced it all and came through it with grace. With Mary we have come through death, we have come through the sorrows and sufferings of adult life, not to a life without pain, but to a life that can hold both at the same time. A life expanded and deepened by experience. We can hold the two seemingly conflicting emotions at the same time. We are big enough for both. We have expanded spiritually. We can experience joy and sorrow at the same time.

As Mary watches her son ascend to heaven, she feels both joy and sorrow. Joy that she had been privileged to know him, to have been his mother, joy that he is going to heaven, and sorrow that he will no longer be physically part of her daily existence. He will still be with her, but in a different way. It is the end of one stage of her life. She must continue to grow bigger every day, holding the joy and the sorrow together in her heart in order to be open to the next stage of her life.

We, too, have grace available to us. Grace that will help us in the tensions of this world. Grace that will not save us from experiencing all the world has to offer, the joys and the pain, but grace that will help us experience both these to the fullest, if only we cooperate with this grace in our life.

> *While he was going and they were gazing up toward heaven, suddenly two men in white robes stood by them. They said, "Men of Galilee, why do you stand looking up toward heaven? This Jesus, who*

*has been taken up from you into heaven,
will come in the same way as you saw
him go into heaven." Then they returned
to Jerusalem . . . All these were constantly devoting themselves to prayer.
—Acts 1:10–12,14*

THIRD GLORIOUS MYSTERY
The Coming of the Spirit at Pentecost

> *And suddenly from heaven there came a sound like the rush of a violent wind, and it filled the entire house where they were sitting. Divided tongues, as of fire, appeared among them, and a tongue rested on each of them. All of them were filled with the Holy Spirit.*
> —*Acts 2:2–4*

It is the spirit that forms us into communities. What would we do without community? How would we ever make it in this life? Mary lost her husband, her son, her family, yet she found community. That's what Pentecost is all about—the mystery of community. How would we ever get through this life without a community? Community sustains us in ways family and friends cannot. When family fails, community is there. How else would Mary have survived first the death of her spouse then the death of her son if she had not had a community?

I have been part of many different forms of community. It still remains a great mystery to me. I have been part of different church communities, having leadership roles in some of these. I have lived in communities, religious and lay. I have been part of small-faith and action-based communities and know the power of these. I live in a small-town community. And I'm part of that wider community of church, the communion of saints. I am part of many communities at the same time. They are all important to me and add significant dimensions to my life.

When tragedies strike, when loved ones die or let you down, when moving from one community to another, community doesn't fail. God never calls us from one community without providing us with another community. God knows our needs, our need for people, a sense of belonging, a sense of worth, and this is truly glorious—more than joyful, glorious.

Community life is not without struggle and conflict. It can take a great deal of work, commitment and bearing with each other to form a community. But it is worth the effort. Once you've had an experience of true community, you are hooked. You keep looking for it wherever your life may take you. My communities have sustained me in so many ways over the years. They have provided support in times of trouble. They have challenged me to grow as we rub elbows and deal with the inevitable conflict that is part of community life. They have given me a sense of belonging, a sense of meaning and purpose.

Mary found herself as not just a part of a community, but an important part. Her son now gone, she became mother to a whole community of believers. She became mother to future generations, successive church communities. From the role of mother of a dead child, she takes on a new role as mother of a community. She bears it well. She holds a place of importance in John's community. Her role is not one of apostle, spreading the Good News, traveling from place to place like Peter and Paul. She doesn't have the prominence that they have, and yet her role is important. Quietly she has an impact on the early church. Her name is not mentioned often in Acts of the Apostles. We hear little about her after the death of her son. No mention is made of her in the epistles, yet her place is established and preserved within the early church community.

Like all women of that time, it's as if she ceased to exist once her husband and son were gone. The testimony of women was not allowed as valid, and yet, as the years passed and people yearned to hear more and more about this man named Jesus, what better source for them to turn to than his mother? I can imagine Mary, growing old with the same grace she had had all her life, the matriarch of her community, sitting by the fire at night and telling her stories over and over again to an audience that never tired of hearing them. In this way she grew old in grace and wisdom, supported by her community and supporting it in turn. She continued to grow in wisdom and grace, possessing in abundance the fruits of the spirit, all necessary to build up life in community. And in this way she serves as an example, a role model, of what it is to grow old with dignity and grace. Jesus cannot provide this for us, having died at such a young age. But Mary can.

All of us are destined to grow old, if we continue living. Growing old is inevitable, but growing in grace as we age is not. Mary can help us with this. Mary was born full of grace and continued to grow in grace as she aged, surrounded by her community.

> *Now there are varieties of gifts, but the same Spirit; and there are varieties of services, but the same Lord; and there are varieties of activities, but it is the same God who activates all of them in*

*everyone. To each is given the manifesta-
tion of the Spirit for the common good.*
—1 Corinthians 12:4–7

FOURTH GLORIOUS MYSTERY
The Assumption

So God created humankind in his image,
in the image of God he created them;
male and female he created them.

God blessed them, and God said to them, "Be
fruitful and multiply, and fill the earth and
subdue it. . . ." God saw everything that he
had made and indeed, it was very good.
—Genesis 1:27–28, 31

There are days when I want to curse this body God has given me. I get so tired of the endless necessity to refuel by eating and sleeping. And it's not enough to eat just anything. There's the need to watch what I eat and try to eat healthily, whatever that means in this world full of chemical additives, preservatives, insecticides, pesticides, growth hormones and steroids. And there are never enough hours in the day to do everything that could be done. Just think, if I could do away with sleep altogether, or at least make three to four hours of sleep suffice instead of eight hours . . . And as a parent, it isn't enough to take care of myself. I also have to see to the physical needs of my children, provide nutritious meals and snacks, care for them when their bodies are ill, see that they get sufficient sleep.

Then there are all the female health problems, enhanced by a poor diet, lack of a regular exercise regimen and lack of sleep—I've had them all. There have been days when given the option of having all these female organs removed, I would have jumped at the chance. Yet when that became a real option, I balked, refused, proving to be yet another one of those difficult, stubborn women holding onto reproductive organs beyond their time of use. Men have their complaints as well, but I lack the ability to recount these from personal experience.

Mary's body was taken up into heaven. It was not allowed to lie in the earth and decay. This indicates the importance of the human body, in general, and the female in specific. As a woman, I am heartened by this. It helps me on those days I feel like cursing that I was born a woman. Those days when I feel trapped in this body, frustrated by the limitations it places on me. In taking Mary's body physically into heaven the human body is dignified, given its rightful place.

There have been times when I longed to be free of this matter we call the flesh. Free to roam in a spirit world, unhindered by physical barriers. Like people who follow new age gnosticism, I want to shed this shell we call a body to be truly free, be free of the battle between spirit and flesh—but true freedom doesn't come from this. Both spirit and flesh are part of God's creation and are good.

Without this body I would not enjoy what it is to eat good food, enjoy good drinks like cappucino or latte. I would not be able to appreciate that first cup of coffee while greeting the day from my porch swing. I would not be able to enjoy the blessings of a good night's sleep or the good feeling of physical exertion. Without this body I would never have known what it is to touch and be touched, to kiss, to make love. And it was within this body that my children grew for the first nine months of their lives. I'm not willing to throw that part of my life away without a fight.

So I am caught in a paradox again. The human body is a source of great pleasure as well as great discomfort and pain. I can't have one without the other. The mystery is that both enhance the other. Just as joy and sorrow exist side by side in this world, enhancing our experience, so pain and pleasure exist side by side in our bodies, enhancing our bodies, glorifying them. Even as we grow older and our bodies become frailer, possessing only a shadow of their former glory, we are being glorified, prepared for our heavenly home.

The human body is not a shell to be discarded, left behind. It is a beautiful part of God's creation. And like all of God's creation, it is good. This is emphasized by Mary's Assumption, whereby the human body is raised with the spirit in equal partnership. God values the body that provided a home for his son, Jesus, and so raised it to be in heaven. God values all of us, body and spirit. Our bodies are truly temples for God's spirit. They are not something to be discarded or abused. And one day we, too, will join in the resurrection of the body with Mary and Jesus.

> *(The rest of the dead did not come to life until the thousand years were ended.) This is the first resurrection. Blessed and holy are those who share in the first resurrection. Over these the second death has no power, but they will be priests of God and of Christ, and they will reign with him a thousand years. —Revelation 20:5–6*

FIFTH GLORIOUS MYSTERY
Mary Is Crowned Queen of Heaven

A great portent appeared in heaven: a woman clothed with the sun, with the moon under her feet, and on her head a crown of twelve stars.—Revelation 12:1

What does it mean to say Mary is Queen of Heaven? She has taken her rightful place among the angels next to her son. This glorious blue sky, the canopy over the earth is now her mantle. She who lived a humble life while on this earth is now queen over all the earth, over all she surveys. How many earthly rulers can say the same thing? The mighty have been cast down and the lowly raised up. It is neither James nor John who sit at Jesus' right hand but his mother, a simple woman. This is a reminder to us that those who are great on earth will not necessarily be great in heaven. It's a reminder of the mystery that things are often not what they appear to be, especially when dealing with matters of the Spirit.

How did this woman who is given so little notice while alive arrive at such a high station in the eyes of the church? It didn't happen overnight, but over the course of years. As the early church grew and developed in their understanding of who Jesus was, a strong tradition of faith developed around his mother, Mary. Certainly the action of the Spirit guided the early church, or else Mary would have remained a person of little acclaim. The Spirit guided the church until Mary was proclaimed Queen of Heaven, recognizing and acknowledging her place of honor in heaven as well as on earth, for all time.

Mother of a son, she became mother of a community and finally mother to a whole church—a community of communities. In her role as mother she remains fully human and yet holds a place of honor above all the angels and the saints. In her own quiet way she helps to put a feminine face on God and reminds us that God is neither male nor female and yet both male and female, encompassing both genders and going beyond. She is a reminder that God cares for us as deeply and even more deeply than a mother cares for her child. She is there for us to call upon as role model—role model for women, for parents, for Christians everywhere. She is aligned with mother earth, majestic, awesome, powerful, yet soft, nurturing and loving. She gives dignity to the simple role of parent.

Things are seldom as they seem. We see Mary rewarded for her years of quiet service. We, too, may take comfort in knowing our deeds of service, our acts of love done quietly without notice are not unrecognized and will not go without reward. We needn't worry about this. Mary wears the crown she forged during her life on this earth. In the same way we may merit crowns about which we are not aware, crowns for the simple acts of service we perform each day. C. S. Lewis in *The Great Divorce* has the main character take a trip to heaven. There he sees a woman dressed as a beautiful queen with a large entourage. When the visitor questions who this woman had been on earth, thinking she must have been a great queen, the response comes that she had simply been a good, kind woman, a mother, someone whom one might never notice. So it will be in heaven. We are all in for a big surprise.

Mary continues in her role of mother/mediator, appearing in simple places to persons of childlike faith, persons of no great social standing in this world—the children of Fatima, Bernadette of Lourdes, Juan Diego, a simple man in Mexico. She supports us, sustains us, nurtures us and always leads us to her son, Jesus. She takes the place that is truly, rightfully hers. In her life of simple goodness and grace, she has truly merited the title of *queen*. In our own way, if we, too, live lives of simple goodness and grace, we may have a share in this kingdom/queendom, each of us wearing the crown we have fashioned throughout our lives on this earth.

> *Then I saw a new heaven and a new earth; for the first heaven and the first earth had passed away. —Revelation 21:1*

PRAYERS OF THE ROSARY

Apostles' Creed

*I believe in God, the Father Almighty, Creator
of heaven and earth; and in Jesus Christ, his
only Son, our Lord, who was conceived by the
Holy Spirit, born of the Virgin Mary, suffered
under Pontius Pilate, was crucified, died,
and was buried. He descended into hell; the
third day he rose again from the dead. He
ascended into heaven and sits at the right
hand of God, the Father Almighty. From
thence he shall come to judge the living and
the dead. I believe in the Holy Spirit, the holy
Catholic Church, the communion of saints,
the forgiveness of sins, the resurrection of the
body, and life everlasting. Amen.*

In so few words we summarize the life of Jesus. Longer
than some obituaries, yet shorter than the Gospels. In
these few lines we hit the highlights of our faith, the highlights of Jesus' life. He was born to die and rise. What a
mystery that is. His greatness lies not in all the miracles
he performed while he lived, great though they were. His
greatness does not lie in his teachings, but in his death
and resurrection. So it is with each of us. What will history remember of us? What will our children remember of
us when they are old and gray? Will they think of us
kindly? Will they remember all we said or did for them?
Or will they simply remember that we loved them?

Jesus' greatness lies in his death and resurrection. It
is a mystery. Why are we born just to die? Jesus was
born not just to die but to redeem death, and in doing so

redeemed life. The world may not remember us after we've died, but there is more to life than this life, more to death than an ending. It is a gateway to new life for those who believe.

It is fitting that the rosary begins with the Apostles' Creed, a recitation of all we believe. Those beliefs are further explored and clarified in the mysteries of the rosary in which, again, we hear of Jesus' birth, his death and resurrection, and life everlasting.

This is our faith, we are proud to profess it in Christ Jesus our Lord. Amen!

Our Father

> *Our Father, who art in heaven, hallowed be your name; your Kingdom come; your will be done on earth as it is in heaven. Give us this day our daily bread; and forgive us our trespasses as we forgive those who trespass against us; and lead us not into temptation, but deliver us from evil. Amen.*

There is no more perfect prayer to be found than the prayer Jesus himself taught us to pray. With all the beautiful prayers to choose from, if I were allowed only one prayer to pray for the rest of my life, this would be the one. It says it all so beautifully. And we continue to write and rewrite prayers, prayers for this occasion and that, prayers for each day, for each hour of each day, when, for me, one suffices. Everything else is but a plethora of words, endless words, when all that is needed is to stand before our God and creator and abandon ourselves to God's will as both Jesus and Mary did.

Hail Mary

Hail Mary, full of grace! the Lord is with you;
blessed are you among women, and blessed is
the fruit of your womb, Jesus. Holy Mary,
Mother of God, pray for us sinners, now and
at the hour of our death. Amen.

Another biblical prayer. I find those prayers that are
rooted in Scripture to be so powerful. It is beautiful and
powerful in its simplicity. "Hail Mary," the words of the
angel Gabriel announcing to Mary her special place of
favor in the eyes of God, preparing her for the role she
would play in salvation. In this simple prayer we
remember over and over again that special event,
Mary's yes to God. We acknowledge the special place
Mary has in history and ask for her prayers. Over and
over again we repeat this like a mantra, acknowledging
Mary and the baby in her womb, Jesus, and asking for
prayers. We say it so many times that it reverberates
throughout our brain, in our memories and throughout
our very being, "Holy Mary, Mother of God, pray for us
sinners, now and at the hour of our death." As we
remember Mary's yes, may our own yes to God rever-
berate throughout our hearts and our lives.

Glory Be

*Glory be to the Father and to the Son and to
the Holy Spirit, as it was in the beginning, is
now and ever shall be. Amen.*

An acclamation of surprise or amazement. When miracles occur in our lives we proclaim—"Praise the Lord!" "Glory be!" In the same way we pause between decades to give praise, shouts of joy to our God and Father, who became one with us through the Son and redeemed us, and who continues to sustain us with his Spirit. We have many good reasons for shouts of joy as we remember the mysteries of our faith through praying the rosary.

Hail Holy Queen

Hail, holy Queen, Mother of Mercy, our life, our sweetness, and our hope! To you do we cry, poor banished children of Eve; to you do we send up our sighs, mourning and weeping in this valley of tears. Turn then, most gracious advocate, thine eyes of mercy toward us, and after this our exile, show unto us the blessed fruit of your womb, Jesus. O clement, O loving, O sweet Virgin Mary.

98

Pray for us, that we may be made worthy of the

s of Christ.